OXFORD PRIMARY SKILLS

MW01098779

Reading and writing

Tamzin Thompson

Unit	Structures	Vocabulary	Skills
Teaching notes page 2			
1 School things page 4	What's this? It's a (pencil case).	pencil case folder notebook paint box glue stick	📖: Cartoon story ✏: Shopping list
2 Toys page 8	The (train) is (green).	puppet boat plane board game dollhouse	📖: Toy store leaflet ✏: Word order Email
3 Talented kids page 12	He's a (dancer). Is she a (singer)?	painter actor basketball player writer dancer	📖: Website factfiles ✏: Capital letters and periods Website
4 In the backyard page 16	Where's (Dad)? He's (under) the (tree).	backyard flower grass bee pond	📖: Cartoon story ✏: Word order Description of a picture
5 Ready for work page 20	This is his (suit). His (shirt) is (white).	sweater suit gloves boots shirt	📖: Factfiles ✏: Short forms Description of a parent
6 On vacation page 24	Where are the (bedrooms)? They're (upstairs).	cabin camper van houseboat bed sofa	📖: Interview ✏: Question forms Interview
7 Funny birds page 28	It's got (long) (legs) and a (long) (neck).	wings feathers tail neck beak	📖: Factfiles ✏: Nouns and adjectives Describing a picture
8 At the café page 32	I like (salad). I don't like (fries).	pizza burger fries ice cream salad	📖: Cartoon story ✏: Short forms Email
9 A cool room page 36	There's a (DVD player).	painting wardrobe bunk beds table DVD player	📖: Website ✏: *There's* or *There are* Website
10 Amazing animals page 40	It can (run) very (fast).	see hear jump sleep play	📖: Factfiles ✏: Adjectives and verbs Description of an animal
More words page 44		Four extra words for each unit	

OXFORD
UNIVERSITY PRESS

Teaching notes

The *Oxford Primary Skills* series is designed to be used alongside a coursebook to develop reading and writing skills, and uses a balance of familiar and new language in different contexts.

Each level of *Reading and writing* is made up of ten units that are designed to be used in order. The texts progress in length and the skills practiced progress in difficulty through the book. The units follow a grammar and vocabulary syllabus designed to be consistent with what the children are learning in their language lessons.

Children starting *Reading and writing 1* should already be familiar with the alphabet and with letter formation and should have covered some reading and writing in their preschool English lessons.

Reading

There is a variety of reading texts through the course to expose children to different types of English in use. Children will be motivated by their ability to read and understand 'real' text types such as websites and magazine articles that have been graded to their level. They will develop the skills of reading and listening for gist and detail, both of which are essential for complete communicative competence.

Some of the text types they will encounter include:
stories, magazine articles, posters, leaflets, websites, factfiles, reports.

Writing

In the Writing section of each unit, the children practice punctuation, syntax and text structuring, and are given the opportunity to write different types of text about themselves closely following a model text that will support them in structuring their writing. Their writing confidence will develop as they find they have written, among other things: emails, descriptions, interviews, lists, diary entries and website profiles.

More words

At the back of the book is an optional section of vocabulary extension exercises that can be used to augment the number of words the children learn in each unit from five to nine. The extra words are consistent with the topic of the unit and can be used by those children who complete the activities in the Writing task at the end of each unit.

It is to be stressed that these words are optional and it is perfectly possible to complete the course without using this additional section.

Unit overview

Each unit is topic-based and the topics are consistent with areas the children will be covering in their English language coursebooks and in other subject areas. The units are structured to offer the children support in developing their reading and writing skills. Every unit follows the same structure:

Reading and Comprehension

pages 1 and 2 of each unit

Five new words are introduced in picture form at the top of the first page. Use the pictures to teach these words which will form the basis for the Vocabulary work in the unit and will also appear in the Reading text.

The Reading text follows the new words. There is also a recorded version of this text on the Teacher's CD.

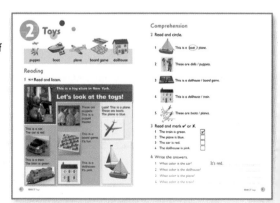

When you start to teach a new text, approach it in three stages: *pre-reading*, *reading for gist*, and *reading for detail*. Explain that children do not have to understand every word to do this. By focusing on the language they do understand, it is possible to guess or use logic to work out the meaning of the rest.

Pre-reading. This stage is about looking for clues to help the children piece together the meaning of the text. This includes looking at the pictures and text style to guess what type of text it is and what it is likely to be about. Ask the children to give suggestions about what they think the text will say before they start to read.

Reading for gist. Play the recording twice while the children follow the text in their books. They do not need to be able to read every word independently, but they should be able to read carefully enough to understand the gist. Ask some simple comprehension questions to ensure they have understood the general points.

Reading for detail. This stage will take place as you go on to the Comprehension page. Go through the first comprehension activity with the class so that the children know what information to look for in the text. Give them time to read the text again to find the answers. Have a class feedback session. Then let the children answer the questions on their own or do the following two exercises together as a class if you prefer.

Vocabulary
page 3 of each unit

The vocabulary exercises give the children the opportunity to practice the new words learned earlier in the unit. The vocabulary items are practiced in the context of simple, graded language structures and alongside other vocabulary items that they are likely to recognize from their coursebook.

Where appropriate, the third exercise on this page gives the children the chance to personalize the language they have been using in a statement about themselves.

At the bottom of the page, you will see directions to the *More words* section for that unit. For those wishing to further extend the children's vocabulary, this is the stage in the unit where these new words should be taught and practiced. This allows the children the option to use them in their writing task on the final page of the unit.

Writing
page 4 of each unit

The Writing page begins with a model text that the children should read. Apply the same approach as for the Reading text.

The children look for clues in the picture and the style of the text for what type of text it might be and what they think they might be asked to write.

Read the text together as a class to see if they were right with their predictions.

Then move on to the exercise following the text. This focuses on a writing skill that will help them to complete the final writing task of the unit. These exercises focus on, among other things:
punctuation, use of capital letters, word order in questions, use of contracted forms, recognizing nouns, adjectives and verbs.

Do feedback as a class before the children move on to the writing task.

The Writing tasks are very well-supported with prompts and gaps so the children are not pushed beyond their level of competence. They are based very closely on the model text that precedes, and the children should be encouraged to refer back to the text you have read together to complete the final exercise of the unit.

For more extensive teaching notes and answer key, refer to www.oup.com/elt/teachersclub/young_learners

1 School things

pencil case   notebook   glue stick   folder   paint box

Reading

1 -01- Read and listen.

Dad: What's this? Is it a toy?
Emily: No, it isn't. Look. It's a schoolbag. And this is a pencil case.

Dad: Is it a folder?
Emily: Yes, it is. And this is a notebook.

Dad: This is a glue stick. OK. What's this?
Emily: It's a paint box. Look. Open the box.

Dad: Open the door, please, Emily.
Emily: OK! Thanks, Dad!

Comprehension

2 Write the letters.

1 This is a notebook. `c`

2 Open the door, please, Emily. ☐

3 This is a glue stick. ☐

4 Open the box. ☐

3 Write *Emily* or *Dad*.

1 Is it a toy? <u>Dad</u>

2 It's a school bag. _____

3 This is a glue stick. _____

4 It's a paint box. _____

4 Read and write *Yes, it is.* or *No, it isn't.*

1  Is this a bag? <u>Yes, it is.</u>

2   Is it a book? _____

3  Is this a paint box? _____

Vocabulary

5 Read and mark ✔ or ✘.

1   It's a pencil.   ☒

2   It's a paint box.   ☐

3   It's a folder.   ☐

4   It's a pencil case.   ☐

5   It's a glue stick.   ☐

6   It's a notebook.   ☐

6 Choose and write.

paint box	glue stick	bag	pencil case
~~folder~~	notebook	pencil	

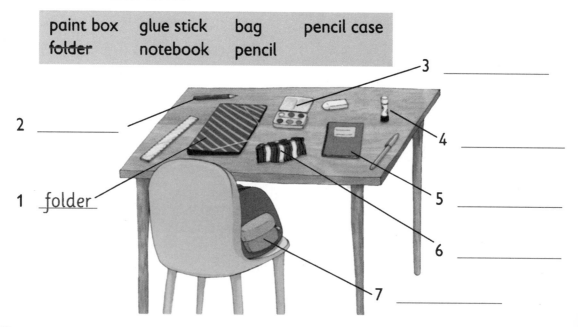

2 _____

1 <u>folder</u>

3 _____

4 _____

5 _____

6 _____

7 _____

More words on page 44

Writing

SCHOOL THINGS	
bag	folder
pencil case	notebook
paint box	eraser
pencil	ruler
pen	glue stick

7 Circle the school things. Write the list.

1 (pen) (pencil) (notebook)   pen pencil notebook

2 folderbageraser   _____

3 rulerpencilcasepaintbox   _____

4 gluestickpenfolder   _____

5 bagnotebookpencil   _____

8 Write a shopping list for your school things.

SCHOOL THINGS

2 Toys

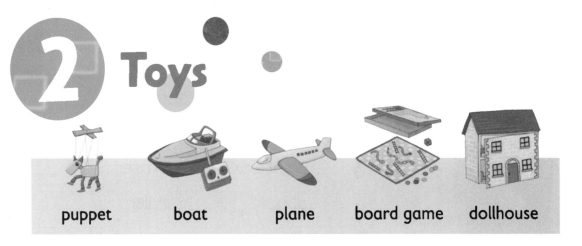

puppet   boat   plane   board game   dollhouse

Reading

1 ◄02► Read and listen.

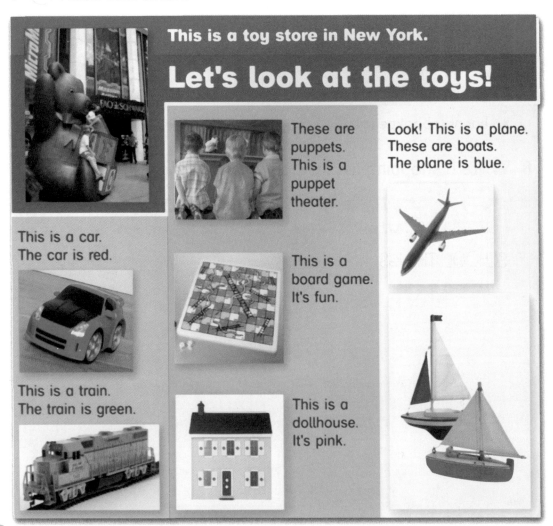

This is a toy store in New York.

Let's look at the toys!

These are puppets. This is a puppet theater.

Look! This is a plane. These are boats. The plane is blue.

This is a car. The car is red.

This is a board game. It's fun.

This is a train. The train is green.

This is a dollhouse. It's pink.

Comprehension

2 Read and circle.

1 This is a (boat) / plane.

2 These are *dolls* / *puppets*.

3 This is a *dollhouse* / *board game*.

4 This is a *dollhouse* / *train*.

5 These are *boats* / *planes*.

3 Read and mark ✔ or ✘.

1 The train is green. ✔

2 The plane is blue. ☐

3 The car is red. ☐

4 The dollhouse is pink. ☐

4 Write the answers.

1 What color is the car? It's red. _____

2 What color is the dollhouse? _____

3 What color is the plane? _____

4 What color is the train? _____

Vocabulary

5 Write the letters.

1 This is a puppet. `b`

2 These are planes. ☐

3 This is a dollhouse. ☐

4 These are boats. ☐

a

b

c

d

6 Complete the sentences.

boat	plane	puzzle
puppet	~~board game~~	car

1 Look! It's a _board game_ .

2 The _____ is red.

3 This is a _____ .

4 The _____ is blue.

5 It's a _____ .

6 This is a _____ .

7 Write about you.

What's your favorite toy? It's a _____ .

More words on page 44

Writing

Hi Emma,

I'm your new email penfriend.
My name's Katie. I'm 6.

My favorite toy is my dollhouse. It's pink.
What's your favorite toy?

Write soon.

Love, Katie

8 Write the words in order.

1 Katie.   name's   My   <u>My name's Katie.</u>

2 is   car.   This   my   _____

3 boat   blue.   My   is   _____

4 my   These   trains.   are   _____

9 Draw or stick a picture of your favorite toy. Write an email to your penfriend.

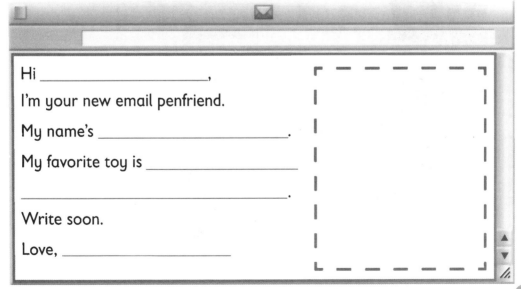

Hi _____ ,
I'm your new email penfriend.

My name's _____ .

My favorite toy is _____
_____ .

Write soon.

Love, _____

3 Talented kids

 painter
 actor
 basketball player
 writer
dancer

Reading

1 03 Read and listen.

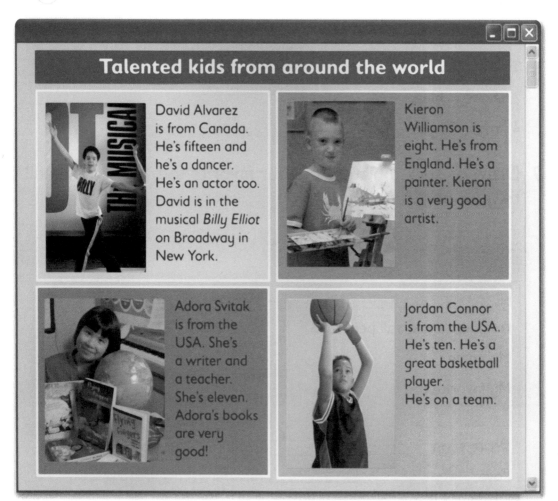

Talented kids from around the world

David Alvarez is from Canada. He's fifteen and he's a dancer. He's an actor too. David is in the musical *Billy Elliot* on Broadway in New York.

Kieron Williamson is eight. He's from England. He's a painter. Kieron is a very good artist.

Adora Svitak is from the USA. She's a writer and a teacher. She's eleven. Adora's books are very good!

Jordan Connor is from the USA. He's ten. He's a great basketball player. He's on a team.

Comprehension

2 Write the letters.

1 He's fifteen and he's a dancer. [c]

2 She's a writer. [ ]

3 He's an actor too. [ ]

4 He's a painter. [ ]

5 He's a basketball player. [ ]

3 Choose and write the names.

| David | Kieron | ~~Adora~~ | Jordan |

1 _Adora_ is a writer.

2 _____ is a basketball player.

3 _____ is in the musical *Billy Elliot*.

4 _____ is eight.

4 Read and write *Yes, he / she is.* or *No, he / she isn't.*

1 Is David a dancer? _Yes, he is._

2 Is Adora a basketball player? _____

3 Is David an actor? _____

4 Is Jordan a writer? _____

5 Is Kieron a painter? _____

Vocabulary

5 Read and circle.

1   Is she a painter? *(Yes, she is.)* / *No, she isn't.*

2   Is he a dancer? *Yes, he is.* / *No, he isn't.*

3   Is she a basketball player? *Yes, she is.* / *No, she isn't.*

4   Is he an actor? *Yes, he is.* / *No, he isn't.*

5   Is he a writer? *Yes, he is.* / *No, he isn't.*

6 Choose and write.

doctor	dancer	~~pilot~~	police officer	basketball player	painter

1 _____ 2 _____ 3 _____

4 _____ 5 _____ 6 pilot

More words on page 45

Writing

Tom Walters

About me:
Hi! My name's Tom. I'm 7. I'm from the USA.

My hero is Lebron James. He's a basketball player. He's 26. He's from the USA. He's great!

7 Write the sentences with capital letters and periods.

1 my name's helen <u>My name's Helen.</u>

2 i'm from korea _____

3 my hero is elijah wood _____

4 i'm from the usa _____

5 she's from mexico _____

8 Draw or glue a picture of you and a picture of your hero. Write about you and your hero.

About me:

Hi! My name's _____.

I'm _____.

I'm from _____.

My hero is _____

_____

_____.

4 In the backyard

backyard   grass   flower   bee   pond

Reading

1 🔘04 Read and listen.

1

Jim: Dad's in the backyard. He's under the tree.

2

Jim: Oh no! Look at the bee! It's on Dad's hat!

3

Emily: The bee isn't on Dad's hat now. It's on his nose!

4

Jim: Dad isn't under the tree now. He's in the flowers.

5

Emily: Where's the bee?
Jim: It's on Dad's hat again.
Emily: Where's Dad?
Jim: He's in the pond!

Comprehension

2 Write the letters.

1 Dad's under the tree.   c

2 The bee is on Dad's nose.   ☐

3 Dad's in the pond.   ☐

4 The bee is on Dad's hat.   ☐

a   b

c   d

3 Put the sentences in the correct order.

a Dad's in the flowers.   ☐

b Dad's under the tree.   1

c Dad's in the pond.   ☐

d The bee is on Dad's nose.   ☐

4 Read and write the answers.

1 Where's Dad? He's <u>under</u> the <u>tree</u> .

2 Where's the bee? It's _____ Dad's _____ .

3 Where's Dad? He's _____ the _____ .

4 Where's the bee? It's _____ Dad's _____ .

5 Where's Dad? He's _____ the _____ .

Vocabulary

5 Read and circle.

1 Look at the (backyard) / grass.

2 It's a *frisbee* / *flower*.

3 Look at the *swing* / *slide*.

4 The *grass* / *tree* is green.

5 This is a *bee* / *tree*.

6 Complete the sentences.

1 Dad is under the _tree_ .

2 Mom is on the _____.

3 My brother is on the _____.

4 The bee is on the _____.

5 The frisbee is in the _____.

7 Look at Exercise 6. Ask and answer.

Where's the bee?   It's on the flower.

More words on page 45

Writing

This is my backyard. Dad is on the grass. Mom is under the tree. My sister is on the slide. The ball is in the tree!

8 Write the words in order.

1 the flower.　is　The bee　on　　 <u>The bee is on the flower.</u>

2 in　is　the garden.　Dad　　 _____

3 is　The frisbee　the tree.　in　 _____

4 on　is　the swing.　She　　 _____

5 the pool.　is　Mom　in　　 _____

6 is　the tree.　under　He　　 _____

9 Draw the items in the picture. Write about the garden.

bee	ball	frisbee

This is my garden.

Mom is _____.

Dad is _____.

The bee is _____.

The ball is _____.

The frisbee is _____.

5 Ready for work

sweater

boots

suit

shirt

gloves

Reading

1 05 Read and listen.

FARMER

This is John. He's a farmer. Look! This is his shirt and these are his pants. His pants are brown. His boots are green.

SOCCER PLAYER

This is Andy. He's a soccer player. These are his shorts. They're red. His T-shirt is blue and white. Look at his gloves. They're white.

WRITER

This is Lucy. She's a writer. This is her suit. It's black. Her shirt is purple.

Comprehension

2 Write the numbers.

1 Look at his gloves.
2 These are his boots.
3 His T-shirt is blue and white.
4 This is her suit.

3 Look and correct the sentences.

1 The soccer player's gloves are red. <u>The soccer player's gloves</u>
<u>are white.</u>

2 The writer's suit is blue. _____

3 The farmer's boots are brown. _____

4 The writer's shirt is yellow. _____

4 Read and write the answers.

1 Are these the soccer player's shoes?   <u>No, they aren't.</u>

2 Is this the farmer's shirt?   _____

3 Are these the soccer player's gloves?   _____

4 Is this the writer's suit?   _____

5 Are these the writer's pants?  _____

Vocabulary

5 Read and circle.

1 Her _dress_ / _skirt_ is pink.
2 Her _boots_ / _gloves_ are yellow.
3 His _coat_ / _shirt_ is white.
4 His _shirt_ / _suit_ is blue.
5 His _boots_ / _shorts_ are blue.
6 His _pants_ / _gloves_ are red.

6 Choose and write.

gloves   sweater   shirt   suit   shorts   skirt   ~~pants~~   socks

1 These are his _pants_____.

2 This is her _____.

3 These are his _____.

4 These are her _____.

5 This is his _____.

6 These are her _____.

7 This is his _____.

8 This is her _____.

More words on page 46

Writing

My Mom by Katie Taylor

This is my mom. She's ready for work. My mom is a doctor. This is her coat. It's white. Her pants are blue. Her shirt is grey. These are her shoes. They're black.

7 Write the sentences using short forms.

1 He is ready for work. _He's ready for work._

2 It is white. _____

3 She is a teacher. _____

4 They are writers. _____

5 I am a farmer. _____

8 Draw or stick a picture of your mom or dad ready for work. Write.

My _____ by _____

_____

This is _____ .

My _____ is a _____ .

This is _____

_____

_____

_____ .

6 On vacation

cabin   camper van   houseboat   bed   sofa

Reading

1 06 **Read and listen.**

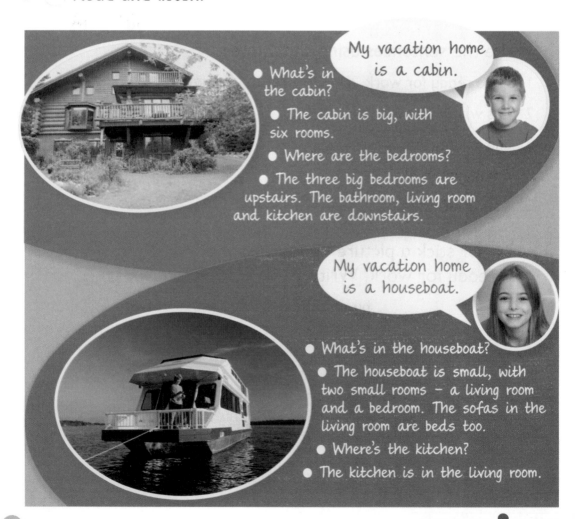

My vacation home is a cabin.

● What's in the cabin?

● The cabin is big, with six rooms.

● Where are the bedrooms?

● The three big bedrooms are upstairs. The bathroom, living room and kitchen are downstairs.

My vacation home is a houseboat.

● What's in the houseboat?

● The houseboat is small, with two small rooms – a living room and a bedroom. The sofas in the living room are beds too.

● Where's the kitchen?

● The kitchen is in the living room.

More words on page 46

Comprehension

2 Read and tick (✔).

two rooms		✔
three bedrooms		
big		
small		
six rooms		

3 Write *cabin* or *houseboat*.

1 The kitchen in the _houseboat_ is in the living room.

2 The bedrooms in the _____ are upstairs.

3 The _____ is big.

4 The _____ is small.

5 The rooms in the _____ are small.

6 The sofas in the _____ are beds too.

4 Read and write *Yes, they are.* or *No, they aren't.*

1 Are the sofas in the houseboat in the living room?   _Yes, they are._

2 Are the bedrooms in the cabin downstairs?   _____

3 Are the rooms in the houseboat big?   _____

4 Are the bedrooms in the cabin big?   _____

Vocabulary

5 Read and circle.

1 This is a (bedroom) / bathroom.

 4 This is a *camper van* / *houseboat.*

2  It's a *cabin* / *camper van.*

 5 It's a *camper van* / *house.*

3 It's a *kitchen* / *bathroom.*

6 Complete the sentences.

dining room	bathroom	living room
kitchen	~~bedroom~~	hall

1 The bed is in the _bedroom_ .
2 The _____ is upstairs.
3 The boy is in the _____.
4 The sofa is in the _____.
5 The stairs are in the _____.
6 The _____ is downstairs.

7 Look at Exercise 6. Ask and answer.

Where is the bed?   It's in the bedroom.

More words on page 46

Writing

This is Billy's camper van.

- **What is your vacation home?**
  A camper van.

- **Is it big?**
  No, it's small.

- **How many rooms does it have?**
  Three — a bedroom, a living room and a bathroom. The kitchen is in the living room.

- **Where are the beds?**
  Two in the bedroom, two sofas in the living room.

8 Write *Where is* or *Where are*.

1 <u>Where are</u> the bedrooms?   4 _____ the living room?

2 _____ your house?   5 _____ the camper vans?

3 _____ the beds?   6 _____ the cabins?

9 Write questions for an interview about Lisa's vacation home.

This is Lisa's houseboat.

- _____?

  A houseboat

- _____?

  No, it's small.

- _____?

  Three — a bedroom, a living room and a bathroom. The kitchen is in the living room.

- _____?

  Three in the bedroom, one sofa in the living room.

7 Funny birds

wings

feathers

beak

neck

tail

Reading

1 07 Read and listen.

The Peacock

The peacock has a blue neck and a yellow beak. It has a very long tail.

The Ostrich

The ostrich is a big bird. It has long legs and it has a long neck. It has a big body and a short tail.

The Kiwi

The kiwi has short legs and a long beak. It doesn't have wings and it doesn't have a tail. It's a funny bird.

Comprehension

2 Label the pictures.

1  _____

2  _____

3  _____

3 Write *ostrich, peacock* or *kiwi*.

1 The _ostrich_ has a long neck.

2 The _____ has a blue neck.

3 The _____ has a long beak.

4 The _____ has a long tail.

5 The _____ doesn't have wings.

4 Read and write *Yes, it does.* or *No, it doesn't.*

1 Does the ostrich have a short neck?   _No, it doesn't._

2 Does the peacock have a blue beak?   _____

3 Does the kiwi have a long beak?   _____

4 Does the ostrich have long legs?   _____

5 Does the peacock have a short tail?   _____

6 Does the kiwi have a tail?   _____

Vocabulary

5 Write the letters.

1 wing   f
2 body
3 feathers
4 neck
5 tail
6 beak
7 head
8 legs

6 Complete the puzzle and find the mystery word.

```
        1
        B  O  D  Y
   2
      E
             3
                I
 4
   T        S
          5
          G
   7    6
      E
          7
          A
   6
```

More words on page 47

Writing

A Funny Bird by Katie Turner

This is the Zongo bird. It's very funny. It has small wings and it has a big beak. It has a short neck. It doesn't have long legs. It has red, blue and yellow feathers.

7 Put the words in the correct boxes.

short	head	tall	feather	small	neck
long	big	beak	tail	wing	funny

Nouns	Adjectives
head	short

8 Draw a picture of a funny bird. Write about your bird.

A Funny Bird

by _____

This is the _____.

It has _____

_____

_____.

8 At the café

 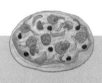 

| burger | pizza | fries | ice cream | salad |

Reading

1 08 Read and listen.

1

Jim: This café is great. Look at the big ice creams. And the pizzas.

Mom: I don't like pizza.

2

Jim: Do you like burgers?

Mom: No, I don't.

3

Jim: Do you like fries?

Mom: No, I don't. I don't like burgers and I don't like fries. They aren't healthy.

4

Jim: Do you like salad?

Mom: Yes, I do. Salad is healthy.

5

Mom: A salad for me, please.

Jim: A salad for me too … And a burger and fries, please! I'm hungry!

Comprehension

2 Write the letters.

1 I like pizza. [b]

2 Do you like burgers? [ ]

3 Look at the big ice creams. [ ]

4 Do you like fries? [ ]

5 Do you like salad? [ ]

[a]
[b]
[c]
[d]
[e]

3 Write *Mom* or *Jim*.

1 I like salad. <u>Mom</u>

2 I like burgers. _____

3 I don't like fries. _____

4 I don't like burgers. _____

5 I like fries. _____

6 I like pizza. _____

4 Read and complete the answers.

1 Are Jim and his mom in a café? <u>Yes,</u> they <u>are</u>.

2 Are the ice creams big? _____ they _____.

3 Are fries healthy? _____ they _____.

4 Is salad healthy? _____ it _____.

5 Are burgers healthy? _____ they _____.

6 Is Jim hungry? _____ he _____.

Vocabulary

5 Read and mark ✔ or ✘.

 1 It's a pizza. ✘

 4 This is rice. ☐

2 These are fries. ☐   5 These are carrots. ☐

3  These are cookies. ☐   6 This is an apple. ☐

6 Complete the sentences.

| pizza | salad | apples | fries | ~~burgers~~ | cookies |

	Tom	Molly	Billy
☺			
☹			

Hi, I'm Tom. I like ¹ <u>burgers</u> . I don't like ² _____.

Hello. I'm Molly. I like ³ _____ . I don't like ⁴ _____.

My name's Billy. I like ⁵ _____ . I don't like ⁶ _____.

7 Write about you.

What do you like?

I like _____ . I don't like _____ .

More words on page 47

Writing

Hi Katie,

Thanks for your email.

I like healthy food. I like salad and I like apples and bananas too. I don't like carrots and I don't like fish. I like pizza.

What do you like? Do you like healthy food?

Write soon.

Love,

Anna

8 Write the sentences using short forms.

1 I do not like apples.   I don't like apples.

2 Burgers are not healthy.   _____

3 Ice cream is not my favorite food.   _____

4 You do not like fries.   _____

5 Bananas are not red.   _____

6 Pizza is not healthy.   _____

9 Write an email to your penfriend. Write about what you like / don't like.

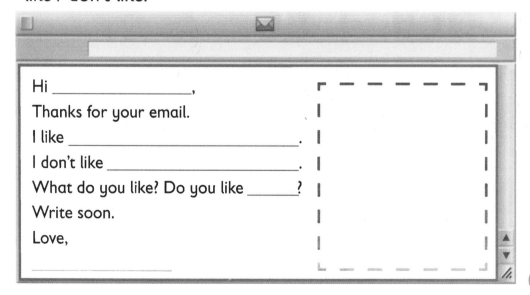

Hi _____,

Thanks for your email.

I like _____.

I don't like _____.

What do you like? Do you like _____?

Write soon.

Love,

9 A cool room

painting

wardrobe

bunk beds

table

DVD player

Reading

1 09 Read and listen.

About the hotel

[Go] ▪ Home ▪ About us ▪ Information ▪ Hotel rooms

There are cool rooms for children in this hotel.

This is a pirate room. There are paintings of boats on the walls. There are two beds in the room. The beds are boats. There's a toy box and there are lots of toys.

There's a wardrobe in the room. There are chairs and there is a table. There are bunk beds, too. There's a TV and there's a DVD player.

Comprehension

2 Read and write the letters.

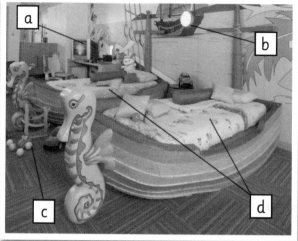

1 There are lots of toys.
  [c]

2 The beds are boats.
  [ ]

3 There's a computer.
  [ ]

4 There are paintings of boats on the walls.
  [ ]

3 Read and mark ✔ or ✗.

1 There are three beds in the room.   [✗]

2 There's a wardrobe in the room.   [ ]

3 There are chairs.   [ ]

4 There are lots of toys.   [ ]

5 There's a computer.   [ ]

6 There's a TV and a DVD player.   [ ]

4 Read and complete the sentences.

| beds | bunk beds | TV | ~~boats~~ | toy box |

1 There are paintings of _boats_ on the walls.

2 The _____ are boats.

3 There are _____ in the room.

4 There's a _____ and there's a DVD player.

5 There's a _____ and there are lots of toys.

Vocabulary

5 Read and circle.

1 This is a *chair* / (*table*.)

2 It's a *pillow* / *painting*.

3 This is a *toy box* / *wardrobe*.

4 This is a *bookcase* / *toy box*.

5 These are *bunk beds* / *toys*.

6 This is a *lamp* / *painting*.

7 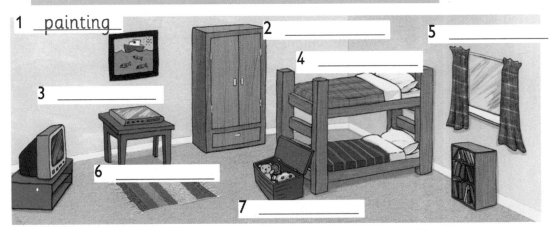 It's a *TV* / *DVD player*.

6 Choose and write.

bunk beds	wardrobe	window	table
~~painting~~	DVD player	toy box	

1 _painting_

2 _____

5 _____

4 _____

3 _____

6 _____

7 _____

7 Write about your room.

My room is great. There's a _____

There are _____

More words on page 48

Writing

This is a great room for children. There are two beds in the room. There's a lamp and there's a CD player. There are toys in the room too!

8 Write 's or *are*.

1 There <u>'s</u> a TV in the room.

2 There _____ two bean bags in the room.

3 There _____ a big wardrobe in the room.

4 There _____ three chairs in the room.

5 There _____ a CD player in the room.

6 There _____ two beds in the room.

9 Write about the hotel room.

There are _____.

There's a _____.

There's a _____.

There's a _____.

There are _____.

10 Amazing animals

see

hear

jump

sleep

play

Reading

1 🔊 Read and listen.

A dolphin can swim and it can jump. It can hear with its ears and it can hear with its mouth too! A dolphin plays lots of games.

This is a bat. It has wings and it can fly. The bat sleeps in the day and it flies at night. It can see at night. It can hear very well too.

An elephant is a very big animal. It can hear with its ears and it can hear with its nose too! It can swim and it can run very fast. But it can't jump!

Comprehension

2 Read and mark ✔ or ✗.

1 The bat has wings.   ☑

2 It flies in the day.   ☐

3 The dolphin can jump.   ☐

4 It doesn't play games.   ☐

5 The elephant can jump.   ☐

6 It is a very big animal.   ☐

3 Write *bat, dolphin* or *elephant*.

1 The _elephant_ can swim and run.

2 The _____ plays lots of games.

3 The _____ sleeps in the day.

4 The _____ can run very fast.

5 The _____ flies at night.

6 The _____ can swim and jump.

4 Read and write *Yes, it can.* or *No, it can't.*

1 Can the bat see at night?   Yes, it can.

2 Can the dolphin fly?   _____

3 Can the elephant jump?   _____

4 Can the bat hear very well?   _____

5 Can the elephant swim?   _____

6 Can the dolphin run?   _____

Vocabulary

5 Read and write the letters.

| a | b | c |

1 It can't see. b

2 It can climb. ☐

3 It can't hear. ☐

4 It can fly. ☐

5 It can swim. ☐

6 It can't sleep. ☐

| d | e | f |

6 Choose and complete the sentences.

1 walk / swim

A fish can _swim_____. It can't _____.

2 run / see

A snake can't _____. It can _____.

3 talk / climb

A monkey can _____. It can't _____.

4 fly / walk

A zebra can _____. It can't _____.

5 swim / hear

A giraffe can _____. It can't _____.

6 run / talk

An elephant can _____. It can't _____.

7 Write about you.

I can _____.

I can't _____.

More words on page 48

Writing

swim   ✔
crawl   ✔
jump   ✗
see at night   ✔
see underwater   ✔

The turtle is an amazing animal. It can swim and it can crawl. It can't jump. It has small eyes, but it can see very well. It can see at night and it can see underwater.

8 Underline the adjectives and circle the action verbs.

1 The turtle is an _amazing_ animal. It can (see) underwater.

2 A snake is very long. It can't walk and it can't run.

3 An elephant is a very big animal. It can run very fast.

4 A dolphin is a clever animal. It can swim and it can jump.

5 A bat is a small animal. It can fly.

9 Write about the gorilla.

walk   ✔
run   ✔
climb   ✔
jump   ✔
swim   ✗
talk   ✗

The gorilla is a very clever animal.
It can _____.
It can _____
_____
_____.
It can't _____
_____
_____
_____.

More words

1 School things

pencil sharpener   crayon   sticker   paint brush

Read and circle.

1 It's a pencil sharpener. *Yes, it is. / No, it isn't.*

2 It's a sticker. *Yes, it is. / No, it isn't.*

3 It's a crayon. *Yes, it is. / No, it isn't.*

4 It's a pencil case. *Yes, it is. / No, it isn't.*

5 It's a paint brush. *Yes, it is. / No, it isn't.*

6 It's a sticker. *Yes, it is. / No, it isn't.*

2 Toys

scooter   tractor   bricks   baby carriage

Write and match.

1 This is a (o t s c e r o) _____.

2 These are (s b i k c r) _____.

3 This is a baby (r i e g r a c a) _____.

4 This is a (r o t r c a t) _____.

3 Talented kids

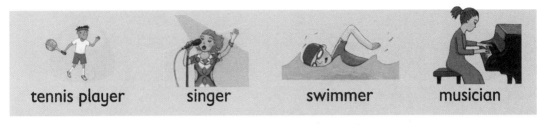

tennis player   singer   swimmer   musician

Read and circle.

1   She's a *tennis player / singer.*

2   He's a *swimmer / tennis player.*

3   She's a *musician / swimmer.*

4   He's a *tennis player / musician.*

4 In the garden

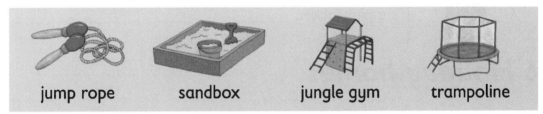

jump rope   sandbox   jungle gym   trampoline

Follow and write.

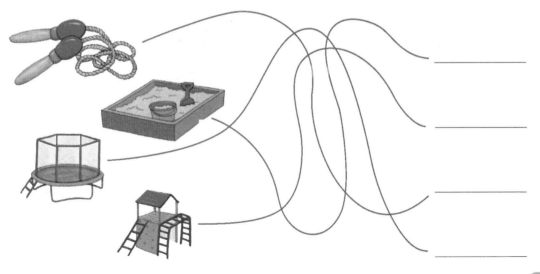

_____

_____

_____

_____

5 Ready for work

jacket   apron   tie   purse

Correct the sentences.

1   It's a red tie. _____

2   It's a blue purse. _____

3   It's a black and white jacket. _____

        _____

4   It's a pink jacket. _____

6 Holiday homes

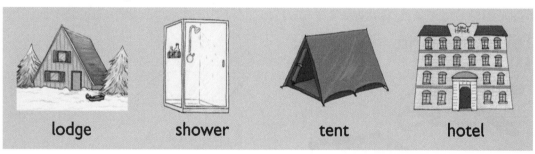

lodge   shower   tent   hotel

Circle four words and write.

1 lodgehotelcabincampervan _____

2 tentcampervanhotelshower _____

3 cabinlodgebedroomupstairs _____

4 showertenthotelcampervan _____

7 Funny birds

fast   slow   funny   scary

Write and match.

1   The ostrich is very (s t a f) _____.

2   This bird is (n u n y f) _____.

3   The penguin is (l o w s) _____.

4   This bird is (c a r y s) _____.

8 At the café

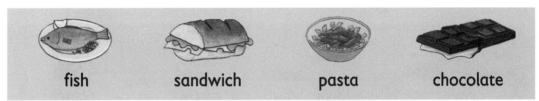

fish   sandwich   pasta   chocolate

Read and circle.

1   My favorite food is *carrots / rice.*

2   I like *fish / carrots.*

3   It's a *burger / sandwich.*

4   I don't like *chocolate / ice cream.*

5   I like *pasta / rice.*

9 A cool room

bookcase   bean bag   phone   computer

Follow and write.

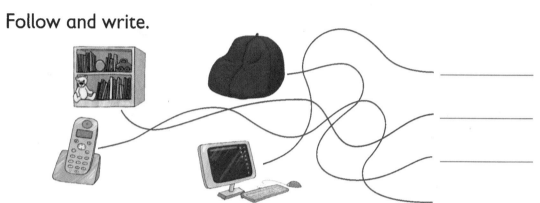

10 Amazing animals

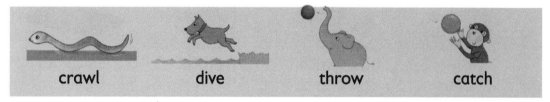

crawl   dive   throw   catch

Read and circle.

1   It can *swim* / *dive*.

2   It can *throw* / *fly*.

3   It can *walk* / *crawl*.

4   It can *fly* / *walk*.

5   It can *dive* / *catch*.